Accounting & Payroll Firm Growth Secrets

How to Attract More of Your Ideal Clients and Keep Them Longer

Mason Duchatschek
Jessica Coffey

Disclaimer

The Publisher and the Authors make no representations or warranties in any form or by any means with respect to the accuracy or completeness of the contents of this work and specifically disclaim all warranties, including (without limitation) warranties of fitness for a particular purpose. No warranty may be created or extended by sales or promotional materials. The advice and strategies contained herein may not be suitable for every situation, person, nonprofit organization, or business. This work is sold with the understanding that the Publisher is not engaged in rendering legal, accounting, or other related professional services. If professional assistance is required, the services of a competent professional person should be sought. Neither the Publisher nor the Authors shall be liable for damages arising therefrom. The fact that an organization or website is referred to in this work as a citation and/or a potential source of further information does not mean that the Authors or the Publisher endorses the information the organization or website may provide or recommendations it may make. In some, but not all, cases, affiliate income may be generated to the Authors from products or services purchased by readers from sites that are referred to in this work. Further, readers should be aware that internet websites listed in this work may have changed or disappeared between when this work was written and when it is read.

Contents

Introduction.. 1

Chapter 1 : The Starting Point.. 3

Chapter 2 : Three Secrets and One Purple Cow........... 18

Chapter 3 : The Numbers Tell the Story.........................31

Chapter 4 : How You (and Your Clients) Win! 51

Chapter 5 : Tools and Training...59

Chapter 6 : The Wrap-Up..68

Chapter 7 : The Workbook 76

Introduction

If you are looking for an unfair advantage for your CPA firm and/or payroll service company, as well as newer and better ways of getting more customers and earning more profit from each of them, then you're in the right place.

Our goal is to help you get the freedom to do what you do best and like to do most, so you can have a solid business, running your way … a business you can do anything you want with.

We also want to help you get the most out of every dollar you invest in your business without putting an unnecessary strain on your resources.

If you feel the secrets we're about to share with you make sense, then we suspect you will have questions at some point and will want to know the simple step-by-step pathway that turns the secrets we're going to share with you into action.

Here's some additional good news: We have added a workbook that will guide you along a simple path, and most of the time-consuming "grunt work" associated with creating marketing content has been done for you!

If you decide this advice isn't for you, at least you won't be caught off guard as the improvements we plan to bring to the accounting and payroll industry in the very near future take hold. At the very least, you will learn about what's coming and how it will impact your industry so you can be prepared for it.

If what you read makes sense and you want to know more about how your accounting firm and/or payroll service can become a strategic partner—and get help executing the ideas mentioned in this book, along with wholesale pricing, product support, and additional training on the products mentioned in this book—simply click on the link labeled "How to Become a Strategic Partner" at https://amohumancapital.com/ and answer the questions on the short questionnaire that is presented. We will follow up with you once your information has been reviewed.

Chapter 1

The Starting Point

We recently surveyed leaders in the accounting and payroll service industry and received results indicating an interest in retaining customers, growing the business without having to sell, and earning more profit. As a result, we have compiled a "how to" book and workbook with step-by-step details. It couldn't be easier unless we came and did it for you, and that would cost thousands of dollars a day.

We promise that you are going to learn our best strategies on how to build a force field around your existing client base, get new account referrals without having to ask, and generate additional revenue at higher profit margins with little or no extra effort—even if you or your staff hate to sell or aren't very good at it. Fair enough?

The first thing we want to mention is that if you've lost important clients, had existing clients try to nickel-and-dime you, or noticed it is harder than ever to get in front of new prospects when they're ready to buy, it's not your fault.

There's a lot of information out there, and it can be confusing. Many times, that information overload keeps you from success. It's OK.

If you've been concerned in the past that you just can't succeed if you make even subtle changes to the way you've always done things, we're here to put those fears to rest. You can do this. You just need the right people to explain it to you.

The bigger CPA firms and payroll companies want you to think you need to "know your place." They want you to believe that to be able to compete with them, you need to merge or make expensive acquisitions, because that's all they know how to do.

Your smaller rivals are hoping you just want to be "happy with what you have," and that you remain complacent so you're not that big of a threat to them either. We're here to tell you they're all wrong. They have their own reason for wanting you to think that, but it's just not right.

If you've ever felt like the larger CPA firms and payroll companies want you to think they have an advantage over you simply because they are so much bigger and have so many more resources than you, you're probably right. They want to keep you discouraged, because they don't benefit when resourceful and competent rivals like you threaten their status quo.

That's what we're here for. We know you have dreams and want to make an impact. We want to show you how to make that happen, so stay with me until the end. You'll be glad you did.

Our goal today is to help two types of people: those who own or manage a CPA firm and those who own or manage a payroll company. With this book, you'll get strategies, tools, and tactics that will help you add more of your ideal clients, increase profit from your existing client base with little or no extra effort, and find out how to outmaneuver and outsmart your rivals before they even realize what happened. As an added bonus, I'll also show you how you can build a force field around your existing client base as well as your expert status and reputation in your market niche.

Just so you know—and we'll talk about this stuff in a bit—we created this thing we call the Human Capital Calculator so you can use your clients' OWN numbers, from work you've ALREADY DONE, to generate a report that will have them literally begging and pleading for help.

Second, when they beg for help, we will show you a way to give them what they are asking for AND generate additional, ongoing residual revenue streams for your firm in a way that requires very little time or effort on your part, because we've already built the systems that practically do all the work for you. How does that sound?

There are a lot of good reasons to be in the accounting or payroll business. Every company needs accounting and payroll services. That's a lot of prospects—and that's a good thing!

Plus, once you have an account, it's a residual income stream that keeps paying you for as long as you can keep a client happy. We get it.

But what happens when a bigger competitor—or even a smaller but more desperate competitor—comes along and undercuts you? Loyalty isn't what it used to be, is it?

As much as we hate to admit it, clients and prospects often tend to view accounting services and payroll services as a commodity. They want it fast. They want it right. They want it cheap. And let's face it, there are a lot of clients that think all you need to do is plug the right numbers in the right columns of some computer program and taxes and payroll get handled. And to a large extent, they're right.

There are lots of companies who can meet those expectations, and it sucks when you find yourself competing against all those other service providers who are willing to keep cutting prices to get new accounts or keep their existing accounts. You know the type.

Want to know how to change that game so it doesn't have to be such a dog-eat-dog industry?

THAT, friend, is EXACTLY what we will walk you through—step by step. We have the answers, and we'll share them with you. It's a win-win scenario for all involved. We're talking about you, us, and all our clients. You'll see.

We're going to walk through strategies, tools, and tactics that will help you add more of your ideal clients, increase profit from your existing client base with little or no extra effort, and find out how to outmaneuver and outsmart your rivals before they ever realize what happened.

Tim Ferris, in his book *The Four Hour Work Week*, said, "If what you're doing isn't working, do the opposite." What's the opposite of becoming a commodity? How can you create and build upon a relationship with your clients? How can you add value above and beyond the minimum services required?

Have you ever noticed how competitive the fast-food industry is? There are so many choices and options. Everywhere you look it seems like there are "dollar menus" and restaurants undercutting each other on price just to get people in the door.

If you're like us, you've probably wondered how anybody can make money selling burgers for a dollar. These companies spend big money on advertising to sell burgers, for example, for next to nothing, and yet more and more fast-food restaurants are doing it. Companies like McDonalds, Burger King, and Hardees have to practically give away their burgers at rock-bottom prices just to respond to market forces and remain competitive.

It sounds kind of like your industry sometimes, doesn't it? Prospects and clients expect better deals or they will go elsewhere. Clients and prospects expect you to practically give away your services, or they will find someone else who will.

To someone who is hungry, a burger from McDonalds, Burger King, or Hardees can do the job. And to a company needing accounting and/or payroll services, there are lots of different service providers who can do those jobs as well.

The big secret is that these restaurants don't just offer burgers. Items like the soft drinks that go along with the burgers bring MUCH higher profit margins—which industry experts claim is around 90%! By adding high-profit-margin products (soft drinks, etc.) that complement their core offering (burgers), these restaurant owners experience prosperity instead of poverty.

We think one of the solutions to growing your business has to do with YOU offering high-profit-margin products and services that complement your core offerings as well. Ideally, those complementary, high-profit-margin products should not be a commodity (like a payroll service) that people can go get anywhere for a cheaper price. Ideally, they should also sell themselves, with little or no effort or marketing expense.

It just so happens we have products your prospects and clients need, and we offer wholesale pricing (along with great margins) to the accounting and payroll firms we agree to work with. In the spirit of full disclosure, if what you are about to read makes sense, we are going to want to talk to you, and we invite you to reach out if you have any questions. The CPA firms and payroll service providers we elect to work with get wholesale pricing on our products, as well as access to "done-for-you" marketing materials and templates, client training videos, and customer support.

Here's the backstory. Mason was in his early 20s when he took his first outside sales job. He was selling tickets for sales training seminars to automotive dealerships in midwestern markets for a very talented but little-known up-and-coming sales trainer.

He made decent money and learned a lot, but when he looks back on it, other than the experience and people he met, it was rough. And that might be an understatement.

He would arrive in a market about 8 weeks before the seminar was supposed to take place, open the yellow pages in the phone book, and write down the phone number of every auto dealership within a 60-mile radius. For those prospects he was able to get in front of, he was giving a memorized presentation, answering objections, and asking for the order. It was old-school selling at its worst. And make no mistake, as a young 22-year-old selling sales training to general managers of car dealerships who almost ALL thought they were God's gift to the automotive sales industry, it was brutal.

When people say they don't like to make cold calls or push products or services—even if they're good products or services—we understand completely! It sucked, and he swore he would NEVER do anything like that again.

The worst part was that after he worked one market, he had to pick up and go do it again in another market starting from scratch. It was a one-time sale. There was no residual income. There was no way to build upon any relationships and trust in a market he had previously served, other than that some of the attendees were willing to serve as references to dealers in other markets.

Even though the pay was great, it was a REALLY tough way to make a living, and at a certain point the money didn't matter. It was a rough road. He had to find a better way. The good news is that he did, and we're about to share it with you.

Jes, on the other hand, spent years in the human resources and recruiting field. She worked with start-up companies as well as various large corporations. The main focus of her work was spending time working with corporate leaders to reduce employee turnover, increase employee engagement, and help the organizations she worked for get the right people in the right jobs.

She experienced firsthand the joys associated with hiring right the first time. She experienced the headaches, hassles, and expenses related to mistakes in hiring. She saw the financial consequences of inefficiency, complacency, and disengaged employees.

One day Mason read an article featuring an interview with Fred Smith, the founder of FedEx. Fred said he used to go to parties and listen to what people complained about, and he encouraged aspiring entrepreneurs to do the same—and start a business if they could figure out a way to fix what people were complaining about.

And you know what Mason heard general managers of auto dealerships complaining about? They complained about the high turnover of salespeople. In fact, that was one of the objections he heard frequently that he halfway bought into. Some general managers had such high turnover they hesitated to invest in training new reps; they had very little confidence the reps would stay long enough for them to recoup the investment made in training them.

General managers told Mason they had used traditional methods and hired good reps. They also admitted that they had used those exact same methods to hire people they wished they hadn't. They expressed frustration because they realized their traditional methods couldn't help them predict, with any degree of certainty, the likelihood that a job applicant was likely to succeed.

The general managers went on to complain about the shortcomings of traditional methods. For example, they knew their hiring decisions were only as sound as the facts on which they were based. But so many applicants lied or embellished on their applications and resumes that they couldn't tell fact from fiction.

They talked about how applicants wouldn't give out names of people as references who would say anything bad about them. They complained that drug tests only proved someone could stay clean for 30 days, and criminal background checks only showed when someone was caught and successfully prosecuted. Criminal background checks were completely incapable of showing who was caught doing things they weren't supposed to be doing if they weren't prosecuted, or they weren't prosecuted successfully—even if they were guilty.

One day, Mason came across an article in *Personal Selling Power* magazine that featured a study by Michigan State University's School of Business on predicting success in the workplace. It that said pre-employment testing was the #1 predictor of future success by a 3-to-1 margin over interviews, past experience, and education.

Mason felt like he had discovered a set of unmet needs. So he decided to take Fred Smith of FedEx's advice.

Mason started researching industrial psychologists across the country and the assessment tools they created for pre-employment assessment purposes, as well as employee development and engagement. And he came across an industrial psychologist by the name of Neal Johnston. He felt Neal's work was exceptional, and he bought the marketing rights to his products and went into business selling them.

Mason's hunch paid off, and he found the pre-employment assessments incredibly easy to sell. All he had to do was get a prospect to try one. His credibility went through the roof, because prospects were amazed by the accuracy of the assessments and how well the reports described them.

And because hiring decisions either solved business problems or created new ones, employers wanted this kind of information on job applicants before they hired them. And sales managers, operations managers, and human resources directors now loved him because he was an ally who could help them identify, retain, and develop the best people. They no longer had to waste their time and resources on people who weren't a good fit.

Mason's mom always said that if you don't think you have the time to do something right the first time, it's even harder to find the time to do it over. It's been Mason's experience that when it comes to hiring, smart business owners and executives also know this to be true. Business owners and executives recognize that the investment in his assessment products is a fraction of the cost of a single hiring mistake, much less a bunch of them, so price isn't usually an objection.

Once assessments became part of his clients' selection process, Mason created a residual revenue stream selling assessment tools just like you have for accounting and payroll services—only the profit margins were and still are WAY better. And because the assessments were unique, they weren't viewed as a commodity and rivals couldn't just undercut him on price.

The usefulness of the assessments went beyond pre-employment testing, too. Decision makers wanted this kind of information to pinpoint opportunities for growth and improved engagement within their existing ranks as well.

Want to learn how to get wholesale pricing on the same exact assessment tools Mason used to build his business? Want access to a "done-for-you" workbook that helps you use the ready-made marketing videos and other promotional content as if you created it yourself? Wouldn't it be nice to have an automated way to do most, if not all, of your selling, client training, and customer service without having to take away from your existing business? <u>It has all been done for you, and we are going to give it to you</u>.

To support the accountants and payroll service providers we want to work with, our videos are like a virtual sales and customer service department that sells and services clients for you, perfectly—24 hours a day, 365 days a year—and reaches an unlimited amount of prospects and clients simultaneously, worldwide. Because the videos are internet-based, little or no effort, expense, or time is required to make that happen either.

Let that sink in. Read that one more time.

We know there are distractions everywhere. But the strategies we're about to share can change your life. We don't want you to miss a single crucial step.

For over 20 years, Mason has worked with and helped small mom-and-pop shops, as well as multibillion-dollar worldwide corporations, solve their common people-related business problems. Specifically, he has helped them reduce employee turnover, maximize employee engagement, reduce labor costs, reduce workers comp costs, reduce shrinkage, and increase sales.

In your accounting and/or payroll business, we suspect you've got some challenges similar to the ones we've faced, like finding consistent ways to get in front of your ideal prospects when they are ready to buy and finding ways to provide such exceptional value, that's so greatly in excess of what your competitors can offer, that current and potential clients can't even imagine doing business with anyone else.

It took Mason years of hard work and hundreds of thousands of dollars to figure all this out through trial and error, but we don't want it to be that way for you. Imagine what your life will be like after you learn how to earn referrals without even having to ask. Imagine opening your email or checking your voice mail to find messages from high-profile people and prominent companies you've never worked with before asking if you can do some of the same remarkable things for them that you've already done for others.

Can you imagine how good it would feel to not have to worry about losing clients, wasting money on advertising, or having to go sell? Can you imagine what it would look like to see the upward arrow on your revenue charts when you look at your own financials, knowing that it took little or no extra effort to accomplish those revenue improvements? How much better would that make things for you?

We figured this out, so you don't have to. If you can follow the simple step-by-step instructions that we have laid out for you and utilize the "done-for-you" marketing resources we've provided and position yourself correctly, you can grow your business.

Chapter 2

Three Secrets and One Purple Cow

We want to share three secrets with YOU that your COMPETITORS will wish we didn't, especially if you APPLY the knowledge we're about to share, regardless of whether or not we ever speak, meet, or do business together. At the very least, we want you to be glad you invested your time with us, and hopefully you think of these little secrets as a gift from us to you.

Secret #1: Some people think the best way to keep your customers is to do a good job for a fair price. The real secret to client retention is to proactively prove that you are attentive to their needs and capable of finding new ways to save your clients far more than they spend on your services.

Clearly, some people believe that all they need to do to keep their clients is do a good job for a fair price. Well, if they're lucky, it may be enough in some cases. However, luck isn't a strategy.

Mason has a client whom he likes, respects, and trusts who was the CEO of a privately held Inc. 100 company, and she referred him to her new CPA. Here's why: She told him that this new CPA had found a little-known way to help another company like hers save hundreds of thousands of dollars PER YEAR in specific tax breaks and credits. She reached out to him and asked if he could help her company do the same, and how much it would cost. He got back to her and the answer was yes, and it would only cost $1,000–$2,000 total. Working together would save her business hundreds of thousands of dollars PER YEAR.

If her old CPA firm didn't know how to capture the same savings, it was certainly a black eye on their professional reputation. If her old CPA DID know how and didn't bother to let her know, that was an even BIGGER black eye because it only proved they weren't paying attention to her company's needs and her company wasn't a priority. The CEO of that Inc. 100 company switched ALL her company's accounting business, which was A LOT, to this new CPA and his firm.

Did her old CPA firm successfully complete her company's tax returns for a fair price in years past? Yes, of course they did. Tax returns are largely viewed as a commodity service because any decent CPA firm can do them, and there are A LOT of CPA firms. In fact, accounting has become such a price-competitive commodity/service that you can now get your taxes done for you at Walmart.

Accounting firms are everywhere. But was doing quality tax returns enough to keep her business? No. A different CPA found multiple ways to save her company far more per year, in real dollars, than her company had spent for accounting services with her old CPA firm in the past. If you ask her, which we have, she will tell you that her NEW CPA firm is proactive, attentive, and always looking for revenue-generating and cost-saving opportunities.

Her new CPA firm proved with their deeds, rather than hollow promises, that she and her company were a priority. Whatever they charge in fees is a fraction of the cost of NOT doing business with them. Her new CPA firm is saving her more than her company spends for accounting services, which makes it BETTER than free.

Takeaway: The *first secret* to client retention is to make fees irrelevant by finding new ways to save clients far more than they spend on your services.

Secret #2: For many salespeople, converting a prospect into a customer without coming off like the unpleasant stereotypes associated with salespeople is hard enough. However, the bigger challenge facing most payroll companies and accounting firms is the double task of being positioned as THE subject matter expert AND getting in front of ideal prospects when those prospects are ready to buy. Some people think that to land more of your ideal, high-profile, and most profitable accounts, you need to be a good networker, marketer, advertiser, and salesperson—or you must hire other people who are. Want to know the truth?

The real *secret (#2)* to landing more of your ideal and most profitable clients is that it's much easier, faster, and less expensive if you can figure out a way to turn your existing clients into advocates and cheerleaders who do all that work FOR you, for FREE, without you having to ask.

So yes, it helps when you can save them more than they spend with you, but you must ALSO proactively PROVE that you are attentive to your client's needs. They need to know you are always paying attention to their business and looking after their best interests as if they were your own.

Do the CPAs at Mason's client's new firm have to go to networking events, spend big bucks on advertising, hire sales reps, or try to do the selling themselves? The answer is NO. Do they have to spend all kinds of dollars on vanity ads trying to tell their marketplace how great they are? NO, because the RESULTS THEY DELIVER speak for themselves, prove their expertise, and solidify their position as trusted advisors and subject matter experts.

The cool thing is that their ideal prospects call THEM when they're ready for better results, and almost all those prospects ask some variation of the same question: Can you do for me what you did for the other client who referred me to you?

Guess what else? The CEO who switched CPA firms is just one of MANY who have become advocates and cheerleaders for her new CPA firm. She's not the only one paying it forward and telling others in her inner circle about them. Her new CPA firm is in the unique position of sorting through ideal prospects who want to become clients—rather than trying to convince cold leads to inquire about becoming clients.

One of the best ways to make that happen is to establish your expert status based on the RESULTS you deliver and DEMONSTRATE proactive attention to your clients' needs while PROVING UNIQUE VALUE and expertise clients don't feel they can get anywhere else.

Takeaway: The *second secret* to landing more of your ideal clients without having to market, sell, or even ask for referrals is to figure out a way to turn your existing clients into your advocates and cheerleaders who do all that work for you, for free, without you having to ask.

It's important to remember that you must **do** something exceptional, remarkable, and unique. It's not enough to do a good job at what others say they can do too.

Secret #3: Some people think the best way to grow your profit is to get more clients. However, an often overlooked secret to growing your firm's revenue—and, more importantly, PROFIT—lies in finding ways to generate additional revenue streams that complement your existing services without interfering with what you currently offer or requiring many, if any, additional man-hours to deliver. As we mentioned earlier, think of it kind of like a hamburger stand deciding to offer fries and a shake with each burger they sell.

We're going to let you in on a little gem. Mason's dad once told him that people don't go to the hardware store because they need a drill. They go to the hardware store because they need a hole. Think about that.

Your clients don't come to you because they need accounting or payroll services. Our clients don't come to us because they need employment tests. Our clients, meaning your clients and our clients, come to us because they need to make their businesses better. They need to reduce expenses and increase revenues.

When it comes to hiring, employers who fail to get all the job-related information they can legally gather about applicants before making an offer are playing Russian roulette without checking all the chambers of the weapon first.

You're in the business-improvement business and so are we. However, we aren't competitors, and we think we may be able to be allies.

It's all about keeping customers longer, getting paid more, and earning more referrals.

When you discover how to add scalable revenue components to your business, revenue increases but the work and man-hours required to gain that additional revenue don't.

If you can do that in a way that positions you as an expert and trusted advisor uniquely qualified to guide your clients in ways others can't or don't, you win. And doors that would otherwise have been closed to you and your firm begin to open.

Recently Mason interviewed the managing partner of a CPA firm in the Midwest who actually ran two separate companies. One was a CPA firm, and the other was a payroll company. During their discussion, the partner made several comments that really stuck out. And we feel compelled to share them with you.

He told Mason that he was struggling to grow his CPA firm because it was so expensive and time-consuming to recruit, hire, and train new accountants. Because the revenue of his firm was limited to the available man-hours of his skilled accountants, he felt like he had kind of hit a ceiling, and couldn't really handle any new clients until he was able to find, hire, and train more new accountants skilled enough to serve his clients properly.

Whenever a CPA on staff quit, that really threw a wrench in his machine and strained his remaining workforce—and jeopardized his relationships with existing clients and the reputation for quality service he had worked so hard to build.

His CPA firm and his payroll company did have some overlap and did share SOME clients, but certainly not all of them. He told Mason that he wanted to offer a payroll service option to existing clients of his CPA firm who needed it, because he knew some of them would go find someone else who would fill that need if he couldn't offer them a viable solution.

He didn't want to open the door for any of them to search for another firm. The reverse was also true—and some of his payroll company clients ultimately became clients of his CPA firm.

He told Mason that his primary focus was on growing the payroll company, because that company had SOFTWARE and SYSTEMS that could perform calculations, generate necessary client reports, print checks, and/or perform direct deposits and didn't rely expensive skilled labor like CPAs. The costs of the software, maintenance, and comparatively unskilled labor required to run those operations were largely fixed and predictable.

In his payroll company, the low variable costs associated with the support of new accounts was negligible, and profitability grew significantly with each new client he added to the company's client list. The revenue was also residual and predictable. He loved that. He could onboard a payroll client once and get paid every pay period like clockwork.

While his reasoning made sense on many levels, he also admitted some downsides. He mentioned that his payroll services were largely viewed by prospects and clients as a necessary commodity that wasn't unique in any way, and because prospects and clients had so many different options and places they could get payroll services done for them, it had become a very price-sensitive and competitive service and his margins were low and shrinking.

What he really needed was a way to generate additional revenue that provided UNIQUE value to clients—something that didn't require additional man-hours by skilled staff—and a way to showcase a proactive attentiveness and genuine concern for the unmet needs of his clients that they were unlikely or unable to get anywhere else.

Takeaway: The *third secret* to landing more of your ideal clients without have to market, sell, or even ask for referrals is to identify unmet client and prospect needs in areas closely related to your existing expertise and services and fill those unmet needs.

If you can figure out a congruent and complementary way to address the unmet needs of your clients without increasing the burden on your skilled staff, create ongoing residual income streams, and do it in a way that positions you and the members of your firm as attentive, proactive subject matter experts, then the bond between you and your client as their trusted advisor becomes almost impenetrable and referrals and profits can grow exponentially.

The obvious question is, how do you do that? We have the answer, and we're going to share it with you. Here's a hint: It isn't doing more of what you've already been doing.

As we mentioned earlier, it's not enough to be great at what you do anymore, and certainly not in a field like yours where there are so many other options for current and potential clients to choose from that all look about the same to the untrained eye.

How can you differentiate? Consider this.

Have you ever heard the term "Purple Cow"? Yes, we said PURPLE Cow. It's a term coined by Seth Godin, who wrote a book with the very same title. In his book, Godin described how he once found himself in a rural area in another part of the world, and as he was traveling, he noticed a brown cow by itself in a field. He described how it caught his attention as it grazed. The sun was reflecting off the dew in the grass, making it look like diamonds in the sunlight. But after a short time traveling the countryside, he had seen so many brown cows that he no longer found a brown cow interesting and thought they all looked the same. In fact, he said brown cows were boring.

Now, can you imagine what would happen if you drove just outside of town and saw a purple cow grazing by the side of the road—something you had never seen before, a totally unique and remarkable creature? If that happened outside any of our towns, there would be a line of cars parked to look at it, take pictures of it, and shoot video. It would be all over social media, and TV helicopters would be hovering overhead in no time flat.

Let's face it: As Godin says, the business world is full of brown cows. Brown cows are boring products and services we can get anywhere. It takes a ton of time and lots of money to convince even one person, much less a bunch of them, that one brown cow is any better than another brown cow. What companies have the unlimited amount of time necessary to convince all their prospects they are different? Who has that much money?

On the other hand, a Purple Cow is a unique and remarkable business or way of doing business that is so extraordinary that it's worth talking about, promoting, and sharing with anyone and everyone willing to listen. It's in a class by itself and is so phenomenal and exciting that people can't help but talk about it, and the story of its mere existence travels everywhere without effort or expense.

It's safe to say that most people look at accounting and payroll companies like brown cows, but it doesn't have to be that way for your firm after today. Is there a way to transform your business into a Purple Cow? We think so. And we think doing so should be a HUGE part of your growth and/or profitability strategy. It is certainly part of ours.

If you're performing accounting and/or payroll services, you know who is hiring and how much of it they're doing. If a company or industry you serve has lots of turnover, you know it. This gives you a HUGE advantage, strategically speaking, if you know what to do next.

Because turnover is expensive, at some point sooner or later your clients will decide to do something about it. And if you can't or don't choose to be part of the solution, they will find someone else who can and will give them the help they need.

Chapter 3

The Numbers Tell the Story

The payroll firm ADP has been flying under the radar with a little-known secret for a few years now, and they've made a wise move because of it. The CPA firm KPMG did the same; they put the industry on notice with their acquisition of Towers Watson, which they announced in July of 2015. By looking more closely at the client base data these firms ALREADY had, from work they had ALREADY DONE, both firms discovered huge opportunities to identify and then address unmet client needs.

For example, say they discovered that they generated 300 W-2s in the previous year for a company with 100 current employees (which is easy to do when they've already got their client's payroll data). It isn't hard to recognize that an employee turnover problem exists for that client. It's like they found their client's itch, with almost no effort or expense, and it was just a question of how to help their client scratch that itch (and other itches like it).

ADP and KPMG expanded into HR services that they now offer to existing clients and made themselves more attractive to potential clients with this one VERY simple and brilliant move. You can, too, and we hope you don't make the strategic error of ignoring it.

Have you ever noticed that Paycor doesn't claim to be just a payroll company? It promotes itself as Paycor "HR and Payroll Services" now. ADP promotes itself as "Payroll, HR and Tax Services." Paychex promotes itself as "Payroll and HR Solutions." And Paycom promotes itself as "HR and Payroll Software." Do you see the common denominator? Do you see the trend?

We also think we've discovered a BETTER way to help you address YOUR clients' unmet HR needs, using BETTER tools in a SMARTER way. And unlike KPMG, you won't have to acquire a company to do it.

So here's our step-by-step formula for finding and scratching YOUR clients' itches while growing and transforming your CPA firm or payroll company into a Purple Cow. And we'll even share and give you access to the tools needed to implement it.

We will also reveal some secrets about how you can compete and leverage YOUR unique relationships and talents in ways that will help you counter your competitors' recent moves and position you and your firm where you need to be in both the near AND distant future.

It's no secret that if you want to be viewed as a trusted advisor, you need to continually provide ADDITIONAL value to your clients. Admittedly, that's not always easy to do, especially if you're stuck doing things the way you've always done them.

Corporate decision makers are harder than ever to reach. The walls around them have grown thicker and taller. On top of that, they are often surrounded by a staff of executives and managers who have a vested interest in making sure their boss doesn't get bad news. And if sharing bad news is inevitable, their goal is to water it down as a means of self-preservation.

Let me introduce you to a step-by-step process that will let YOUR CLIENTS' OWN NUMBERS tell their story, the truthful story and the whole story, in a way that positions YOU as the authority, the trusted advisor, and the ONE expert who TRULY understands their unique situation and can help them WHEN and WHERE they need it most.

Dr. Tony Alessandra, who over the years has proven to be one of our favorite authors and speakers, often says, "A doctor who writes a prescription without an analysis is performing malpractice."

So … we are going to do three things.

First, we will show you how we can help YOU help YOUR clients analyze some indicators in THEIR businesses in ways they've NEVER seen before. You should already have these numbers and be able to get them easily—if you don't know them off the top of your head. Once you do that, you can show your clients what they're doing well and where they can easily improve, in specific areas and in MEASURABLE ways.

The analysis tool we will share with you, called the Human Capital Calculator, is a proprietary tool we created for exclusive use with our clients and strategic partners. We built it from scratch. There is a short version that explores specific costs related to employee turnover and employee engagement, as well as projected rewards and cost savings tied to the achievement of measurable improvement goals.

The beautiful part is that you can use YOUR CLIENT COMPANY'S real data to create incredibly accurate and relevant insights they can use RIGHT NOW to make better decisions for their company, faster— beginning today.

There is also a long version of this tool that explores missed opportunities and areas for improvement related to workers' comp, employee theft, and sales performance. But for today, we will stick with the short version.

It's fair to say that almost every one of your clients will have opportunities for some degree of improvement. Of course, certain opportunities will be greater in some companies than in others, for a variety of reasons. Today we will show you how to get them begging for your help in a way that makes any of your fees-for-service a nonissue.

Next, we will give you a sneak peek into the tools and step-by-step best practices being used right now by businesses both small and large, across industry lines, to implement the performance-improvement secrets I'm going to share with you—which you, in turn, will be able to share with your clients. How does that sound?

As we mentioned before, if you're performing accounting or payroll services, you know who is hiring and how much of it they're doing. And if a company or industry you serve has lots of turnover, you know it. This gives you a HUGE advantage, strategically speaking, if you know what to do next.

Turnover is expensive, and at some point sooner or later, it's likely that your clients will decide to do something about it. If you can't or don't choose to be part of the solution, they will find someone else who will give them the help they need.

In Jim Collins's best-selling book *Good to Great*, he said the most important thing any business can do is get the right people on the bus and get the wrong people off the bus. More importantly, he said it is critical to get the right people in the right seats on the bus. The bus of course, is their business.

Collins published his book in 2001, and people are still talking about it in seminars and board rooms all over the world. Why? It's because he was right, and everyone knows it. What people who read his book DON'T know is HOW TO DO IT and WHAT TOOLS ARE NEEDED, because his book DIDN'T give those secrets away.

The second half of the book *People Matter Most* on Amazon.com DOES give away those secrets. It says EXACTLY how to do it—and even reveals the tools that are necessary. We know this because Mason WROTE that book. But you don't have to spend the money to buy that book or invest the time to read it, because we're going to tell you exactly what you need to know here. (Bonus: There is a link in Section 2 of Chapter 7 of this book where you can download the PDF of *People Matter Most* for FREE.)

How critical is it for a company to get the right people on their bus and into the right seats? Specifically, in terms of dollars and cents, how big of a deal is it? How much can an organization save if they do it well? And how much will the organization suffer if they don't?

Now there's an easy way to find out. Here it is. Basically, we enter information clients should know off the top of their head, or be able to access easily, into our proprietary Human Capital Calculator. It's important to use a client's REAL numbers so THEY know the REAL rewards that are tied to their strategic decisions and tactical courses of action.

Once the data is entered, the Human Capital Calculator will provide a custom report showcasing real costs—as well as potential savings tied to improvements—associated with employee turnover and employee engagement. The longer version of the report can also address issues related to workers' compensation, shrinkage/employee theft, client retention, and new account acquisition. Let's take a quick look at how to evaluate the details of the report related to EMPLOYEE TURNOVER.

How much does it cost a company, specifically, when they put the wrong people in the wrong positions and the employees leave? This tool (which we make available to our strategic partners in the accounting/payroll industry) will help determine the dollar cost of employee turnover and calculate the financial rewards that are tied to achieving targeted and measurable improvement goals.

We simply plug in things like how many people a prospect or client lost, how many they have left, and their average salaries, and the Human Capital Calculator report will tell us how much it costs that prospect or client each time they lose a person, as well as the total cost of losing all the people they lost for the year. It will even calculate the potential savings they could recover based on their ability to achieve their goals for reducing turnover.

For example, here's how it works using data we plugged into the calculator for a sample manufacturing company with 150 employees and a payroll of $5.5 million, not including overtime costs. As shown below, there are three tiers or categories of employees. We also entered a goal of reducing turnover by 25% in this example.

(# of w2's) - (# of employees)	* Avg. Annual Salary	* Turnover Expense Rate	Total
35 - 25	X $50,000	* 21%	$105,000

Tier 2 - For positions paying less than $30,000/yr

(# of w2's) - (# of employees)	* Avg. Annual Salary	* Turnover Expense Rate	Total
300 - 120	X $25,000	* 16%	$720,000

Tier 3 - For executives and physicians

(# of w2's) - (# of employees)	* Avg. Annual Salary	* Turnover Expense Rate	Total
6 - 5	X $150,000	* 182%	$273,000

Total Turnover Cost = $1,098,000

Total Turnover Savings = $274,500

STRATEGIES

1. Improve 'Job Match' when hiring (skill, attitude, behavior)
2. Improve retention (minimize conflict and drama)

Tier 1 is composed of all the people who are not executives or physicians but are earning more than $30,000 a year as technicians, salespeople, managers, and other professionals. According to various researchers, it costs approximately 21% of their average salary to replace each person lost in these roles. That's what we call the turnover expense rate.

Tier 2 is composed of hourly and production employees typically making less than $30,000 a year. According to various researchers, it costs about 16% of their average salary to replace each person lost in these positions.

Tier 3 is composed of executives and/or physicians, and various researchers estimate that the cost to replace each one of these people who is lost ranges from 150% to 213% of their average annual salary. In this example, we picked a turnover expense rate right in the middle at 182%.

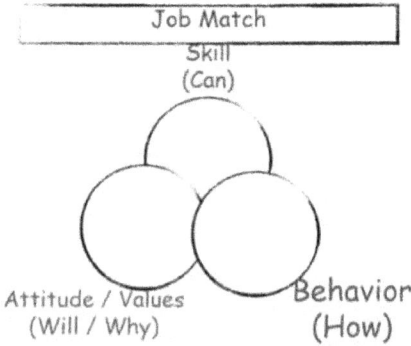

Of course, if a client has done internal turnover cost studies, the calculator will allow us to plug in their own custom turnover expense rates for each of these tiers of employees. To calculate the cost of turnover for each of these tiers, the calculator simply subtracts the number of current employees from the number of W-2s produced last year, and then multiplies that number by the average salary for people in that tier. Finally, the remaining number is multiplied by the turnover expense rate for people in each of the tiers to calculate the cost of turnover for that tier.

When we add up the total cost of turnover for each of the tiers, then we know how much employee turnover costs that business each year. In this example, the total cost of turnover is $1,098,000. Since we plugged in a goal of achieving a 25% reduction in turnover, the report indicates a potential savings of $274,500 per year if they can pull that off—and more if that company can do better! (That adds up to $2,745,000 over 10 years if there is a way to reduce turnover by something as meager as 25% and maintain those improvements.)

Below the data, you'll see some of the suggested strategies and tactics for helping that company achieve their targeted turnover reduction goals.

Strategy number 1 is improving job match by making sure people have the skills, attitude, and personality required by the job. People don't want to stay in positions that rub them the wrong way and cause friction.

As our friend and colleague Hank Epstein, a consultant from Washington, Missouri, often says, "Everyone has two jobs. The first job is doing what their boss expects, and the other is protecting their job."

Employees want to look good, and it's hard when they are in a role that requires them to act like or pretend to be something they aren't.

Strategy number 2 is to improve retention by minimizing unnecessary conflict and drama at work, particularly between individuals and their supervisors, where they often feel most powerless and frustrated. Matching people to the right supervisors can be a highly effective retention strategy as well.

Leadership Match

Team
Leader

↓

Team Member

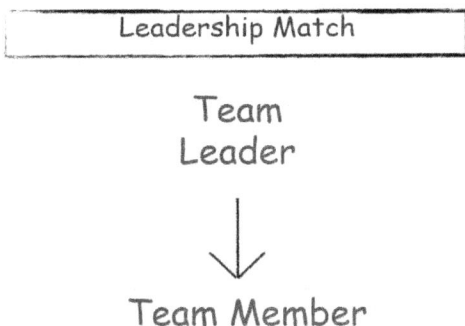

If we examine the Human Capital Calculator report summary, it's all there for you and, more importantly, for your clients to see. Underneath the $274,500 ANNUAL savings they get if they can drop turnover by 25% it shows you the number of employees and W-2s, the annual turnover costs, and the target amount they selected for improvement, in this case 25%.

Use of this section of the tool demonstrates the importance of hiring and keeping the right people in the right positions, and eliminating the kind of drama and conflict that drives them away and/or makes them disengaged and unproductive.

Can you see how giving your clients the ability to reduce risks and match people to jobs and to team leaders they will work well with could easily reduce turnover, and do so dramatically? With the right strategies, best practices, and tools, hitting these achievement goals—or even higher ones—doesn't have to be that hard.

The Human Capital Calculator report also reveals some of the best strategies and tactics for reducing labor costs. Reducing labor costs typically results from hiring people who match the demands of a job, minimizing conflict and drama between existing employees, and improving communication between team leaders and team members.

Reducing turnover costs is a big win for your clients. Improving employee engagement and reducing labor costs can be even a bigger win. Let's take a look at an example.

An easy way to reduce labor costs is to improve employee engagement, increase the discretionary effort of employees, and get more work accomplished with fewer people. When you look at employee engagement statistics, you'll find that there is a lot of room for improvement for most companies.

👥 REDUCE LABOR COSTS / INCREASE LABOR ROI

Percentage of employees:

- **Actively Engaged:** 31.5% (enthusiastic, committed, productive, innovative)
- **Not Engaged:** 52% (checked out, sleepwalk through the day)
- **Actively Disengaged:** 16.5% (destructive, disruptive, hostile)

*Estimates based Gallup polling data of 6,976 adults working for employers

Option 1. For Salaried and Hourly Employees (excluding overtime)

What is the BEST POSSIBLE EFFORT that the AVERAGE employee could contribute EACH DAY? **100%**

CURRENT Discretionary Effort Average **40%** X Annual Labor Cost **$5,500,000** = **$2,200,000**

PROJECTED Discretionary Effort Average **80%** X Annual Labor Cost **$5,500,000** = **$4,400,000**

Projected Labor Resources	- Current Labor Resources	(Additional Labor Savings/Resources Available)
$4,400,000	-$2,200,000	$2,200,000

In a Gallup poll of 6,976 adults working for employers, it was reported that 31.5% of employees were actively engaged, enthusiastic, productive, and innovative. The same poll revealed that 52% were NOT engaged, were checked out, and were sleepwalking through the day. It also showed that 16.5% were actively DISENGAGED, destructive, disruptive, and hostile.

In the following example of a company with an annual payroll of $5,500,000, the person filling out the calculator was asked to estimate the CURRENT discretionary effort of the average employee, and using the data from the Gallup poll as a baseline, they estimated the answer was about 40%.

That meant that the company was paying for $5,500,000 worth of labor but was only getting 40% of that labor in return, which amounts to $2,200,000 worth of work.

The question was then asked, what would happen if there were ways to increase the discretionary effort of the average employee from 40% to 80%? If that could be accomplished, then the payoff would be an additional $2,200,000 per year.

As a matter of strategy, if a company has the ability to match people to their ideal jobs, then employees will be able to do what they do best and like to do most, and will accomplish MUCH more than they would if they continued sleepwalking through the day, sabotaging the company, or barely doing enough to avoid being fired.

When employees get matched to ideal supervisors, and conflicts and drama are minimized, workers can and should be much more likely to accomplish more work every day. The Human Capital Calculator shows the payoff (in dollars and cents) tied to improvements in matching applicants to jobs and the supervisors they work for.

Not only does this tool show the savings tied to reductions in employee turnover, but it also shows the savings that can be captured by improvements in employee engagement. When prospects can see real savings using their real numbers and achievable goals using time-tested tools and strategies, you will have them begging you for your help.

When people become that much more productive, we can add in the savings of overtime costs, which for this sample company is $250,000 per year. That brings the total savings tied to the improvement goals up to $2,450,000 per year.

Putting the right people in the right seats, identifying and filling performance-limiting gaps, and reducing drama and conflict in the workplace are just a few examples of additional ways you would now be able to support your clients.

The right people... in the right seats.

What problems can't be solved?

If your clients' businesses are bigger than the one we've shown in the example, their savings (or losses) would likely be much bigger numbers, but they don't have to worry about estimating, because we can plug in their EXACT numbers and provide detailed and customized reports specifically for you and your clients' companies.

Can you imagine how valuable it would be for your clients to have their own customized Human Capital Calculator analysis for each of their businesses? Suppose you entered a client's REAL numbers into the Human Capital Calculator and they realized the status quo was costing them hundreds of thousands or maybe even millions of dollars a year.

It's also reasonable to expect those losses would continue to mount year after year until something changed. So it would be like helping your clients realize they had an embezzler on their staff who was currently stealing and making more plans to continue stealing from the company year after year until something was done about it. If they knew they had someone embezzling that kind of money each year, how long do you think they would wait to fix it?

Remember when we told you we would teach you how to get in front of prospects when they are ready to buy? Here's how that works.

Suppose you crossed the street, got hit by a bus, and were miraculously able to survive. Rest assured the first paramedic and ambulance to arrive wouldn't have to sell you on the idea of going to the hospital.

You'd be begging them to save you and hoping they could get you to the nearest hospital ASAP. You'd be ready to buy their paramedic and ambulance services RIGHT THEN, and cost would not be an issue.

Well, the Human Capital Calculator has a similar effect, and prospects who didn't see a need for help before suddenly become READY TO BUY the MOMENT after the truth behind the numbers revealed in their report hits them like a bus, figuratively speaking.

And make no mistake, when you look at costs and potential savings beyond the turnover costs, along with employee engagement, and examine the other issues addressed by the Human Capital Calculator, like employee theft, safety, and sales, the impact becomes undeniable.

Once clients see the results of the Human Capital Calculator, they must ask themselves what they're going to do about this information. And THIS is where your opportunity lies. This is where we have a system in place that can help you help your clients IDENTIFY and ADDRESS their unmet needs.

Takeaway: As we've said before, if what we've shared makes sense, then you can build a force field around your clients, get referrals without asking, and reap the long-term rewards of ongoing residual income streams for YEARS to come.

If you're like most people, you've got one big obstacle. It's resistance to change, and it's a cancer we see plaguing far too many payroll and accounting firms. Of course, they don't call it cancer or even think of it as such.

The late Tom Travisano was the co-author of the book *You're Working Too Hard to Make the Sale*, and he once said something that we want to share with you. He said, "Do you know why cancer kills so many people? In far too many situations, people ignore their symptoms. They ignore the signs until the pain is so great they can't take it anymore, and when they finally do go to see a doctor, it's too late to do anything about it, or they suffer through other treatments that are far worse and more painful than was necessary. Had they just recognized and acknowledged the issues up front and taken the right steps when they should have, things might have turned out differently for many of them."

Make no mistake, your best clients are your rivals' best prospects, and they are actively being pursued. And if you aren't at least anticipating—and ideally addressing—their emerging needs, you'll have nobody else to blame WHEN, NOT IF, they go elsewhere. And, of course, it's always easier to keep an existing client than get a new one.

When it comes to revenue, and more importantly PROFIT growth, it's easy to serve existing clients with the new things they want and need because they already know, like, and trust you. When it comes to new account acquisition, it's better to be the company that clients run TO because you CAN meet their needs than it is to be the one they run FROM because you DON'T.

Chapter 4

How You (and Your Clients) Win!

What would a strategic partnership look like? What's in it for you? What's in it for your clients?

First, we want to help you build your business. It builds ours too and provides exceptional value to your clients, so everyone wins. We are willing to help you create white label reports for your clients that look like they came directly from you, not us, using our Human Capital Calculator FOR FREE so your clients can see—in real dollars, right now—what opportunities can be seized or lost depending on what, if anything, they choose to do differently when it comes to selecting, developing, and retaining top talent in their organizations.

If all you did was give each of your clients a copy of their own customized Human Capital Calculator report, using their real numbers, at least you would demonstrate with your actions, and not just words, that you are proactively paying attention to your clients' needs and looking out for their best interests.

That's the kind of service that builds a FORCE FIELD around your client base and generates referrals to new clients without you having to ask. If you want to keep things real, consider this. How much would it cost to lose your best client? How about a few of your best clients? Why risk losing ANY of them when it is so easy and inexpensive to keep them?

After your clients review their report and they realize their status quo is no longer acceptable when it comes to employee retention, engagement, and performance, we have what we think (and you may agree) is a better way to help you help your clients do what Collins told people to do in his book *Good to Great* but didn't say how. And that is getting the right people on the bus and into the right seats. But how do you do that?

You start by finding out who is on the bus and determining what the seats look like, figuratively speaking. We suggest that businesses take inventory of their existing staff by administering a Personality Plus behavioral assessment to each and every one of their current employees, so they know who they have on their bus and what each person brings to the table.

Hiring Suite® (Web) Version 1.5
Copyright 2000-2005, Advanced Psychometrics, Inc.

EXTENDED REPORT

The electronic and/or printed booklet and this report are prepared for general use throughout the United States. Our legal counsel has advised us that all questions comply with existing Federal employment laws including the Americans With Disabilities Act. However, various laws and related statutes and interpretations of them change frequently. For this reason, neither Advanced Psychometrics Incorporated nor its counsel assume responsibility for any questions included in the electronic and/or printed booklet which may violate local, state, and/or Federal laws. Users should consult their counsel about any legal concerns they may have with respect to use of these results. These results should not be construed as a recommendation to have/not have this individual in a preemployment situation. The administrator must check previous work records, job skills required, current status, and personal references. Where safety of other workers is the public is of concern, a drug test should be administered, criminal background checks obtained, and a physical should be administered by a qualified physician. The scoring mechanism utilized to produce this report does not measure political opinions or whether an individual has a tendency to commit violent acts, has any type of psychotic condition, or is sexually deviant, and can not be used for purposes of identifying political views or predicting these types of behaviors/conditions.

Name:	**PERFECT, POLLY**	Phone:	**555-555-1234**
Address:	**123 Anywhere Street**	Work Phone:	
City:	**Oshkosh**		
County:		Position:	**Secretary**
State:	**WI**	Administrator:	**Frank**
ZIP:	**75543**	Date Administered:	**5/3/2006**
		Date Graded:	**5/3/2006**

PERSONALITY PLUS®

The distortion scale deals with how candid and frank the respondent was while taking this assessment. The range for this scale is 1 to 9, with higher scores suggesting greater candor. The letter I indicates that the test is invalid due to too many unanswered questions in Section II.

The distortion score on this assessment is 7.

Organization:	10	Tension:	5
Sensitivity:	7	Probing Level:	6
Imagination:	6	Social Need:	8
Flexibility:	3	Assertive:	8
Recognition:	5	Competitive:	4

Custom profiles can be created for each position in your company by analyzing top performers. There is no additional charge for this service.

These numeric scores represent how Polly compared to **national success patterns** for each job. The closer to 100 the score, the better she fits the demands of that job.

Custom Profiles

Sr. Prog	=85	=	=	=	=

National Generic Patterns

Sales		Management		Office		Service		Misc	
retail	=97	warehse	=91	bookkepr	=94	hotelclk	=91	hrmgr	=94
outsales	=73	acctcomp	=97	secrtary	=100	engineer	=97	trkdrivr	=88
insales	=82	execmgmt	=82	recpntst	=97	autoserv	=91	banktell	=100
countsls	=97	salesmgr	=82	officemgr	=97	custserv	=94	apartmgr	=94
automtve	=88	financial	=97	fileclrk	=91	delivery	=91	leaseagt	=79
tellmkt	=85	techncal	=85	dataentr	=91	tchnical	=85	warehous	=91

The Personality Plus assessment was developed by Neal Johnston, a brilliant industrial psychologist, and unlike background checks and other services viewed as commodities, it is proprietary. Companies cannot get the Personality Plus except through the strategic partners whom we authorize to work with us.

By the way, we believe it is SUPER important for anyone we partner with to remain in control of THEIR client relationships. That means it is ENTIRELY up to you and any other payroll and accounting firms we partner with to decide if clients even know we exist behind the scenes or not.

What that means is if we decide to work together, the companies you work with are YOUR clients and this is YOUR show. We take pride in our ability to help you serve them without interfering with what you're already doing. Here's the bottom line: If or when we ever work together, we can help you support your clients behind the scenes as much or as little as you need us to.

The TYPICAL investment for an end user or client to administer and score each Personality Plus assessment usually ranges in price, starting at $60 per person when clients invest in large quantities and going up from there. So for a company like the one in the previous example with 150 employees, they should expect to invest about $9,000 to assess their entire staff, which by comparison is only about HALF of what most companies pay ONE SINGLE unskilled hourly worker over a year to mop floors, vacuum, and take out trash.

With the release of this book, we will have a special arrangement set up for you and any other strategic partners we choose to work with in the accounting and payroll industry. Because behavior that is rewarded gets repeated and we know it will take bold moves to compete AND WIN against our common rivals, we're willing to make a working relationship between your company and ours WELL worth everyone's while.

In fact, if you mention our book when we speak, our company will cover the costs associated with administering the Personality Plus assessment to every current employee in each company for which you complete a Human Capital Calculator report that wants to take inventory of their existing staff using the Personality Plus.

What does that mean for you? Well, it doesn't mean you need to pass off all those savings to your clients. Feel free to charge full price or half price and keep the up-front revenue. Or if you're feeling generous, pass on the savings entirely to your clients. It's your call.

We bet you're wondering what this could look like. Well, here's an example.

Recently we were working with a company with 1,100 employees and VERY conservative improvement goals, and by using the actual numbers entered into the Human Capital Calculator directly from their payroll data, the report showed them savings opportunities of over $9,125,353 dollars per year if they were even able to hit SOME of the lowest improvement targets they set for themselves.

The investment of assessing all 1,100 employees at $60 each would have only been $66,000, and that was a VERY small investment compared to the ROI of over $9.1 MILLION that their own internal data suggested was not only possible but probable!

So if that had been YOUR client, you could have charged them the $66,000 and kept it all; or if you felt generous, you could have given them half off and kept $33,000 all to yourself, because we wouldn't charge you for the assessments necessary to score your clients' existing staff.

Or if you REALLY wanted to build a force field around your client base, you could tell them you would cover the entire cost of their project—and watch their loyalty grow. Watch the referrals come in.

That means you could create the opportunity for SIGNIFICANT chunks of up-front revenue to your business without having to tie up a bunch of time or other resources. Why? Because the system almost runs itself once it is set up. The time it takes to execute what we just described for a client is usually about 20 minutes total. Do that for a bunch of your clients and that could be a huge injection of up-front revenue —or the kind of good will that inspires more loyalty and referrals—with almost no extra effort.

Takeaway: You can control the amount of up-front revenue for your growing company—all that revenue for just 20 minutes of work.

Chapter 5

Tools and Training

It's vital to help clients learn what the seats on their bus look like. A custom job pattern can be created for every position in their company if they provide a list of names containing the top performers in each position.

RETAIL SALESPERSON

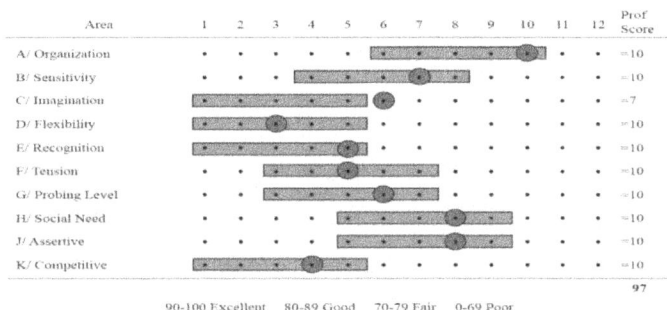

Area	1	2	3	4	5	6	7	8	9	10	11	12	Prof Score
A/ Organization													=10
B/ Sensitivity													=10
C/ Imagination													=7
D/ Flexibility													=10
E/ Recognition													=10
F/ Tension													=10
G/ Probing Level													=10
H/ Social Need													=10
J/ Assertive													=10
K/ Competitive													=10

97

90-100 Excellent   80-89 Good   70-79 Fair   0-69 Poor

The red dots represent Polly on a scale from 1 to 12 for each trait.

The green zones represent the ideal range for each trait in each specific job position.

Regarding the "Prof Score," every time Polly fell within the green zone, she earned 10 points. Each time Polly fell outside the green zone, she earned fewer points. The farther from the green zone, the fewer points she earned.

Polly earned a total score of 97 out of 100 for RETAIL SALESPERSON.

It normally costs $500 to create a custom pattern for a position. However, if we decide to work together, we won't charge your firm to create those custom job patterns for your clients either. That doesn't mean YOU can't charge them and keep all the revenue for your firm instead.

Think about it. If you have a client company that has 7 different key positions, it would normally require an additional one-time investment of $3,500 to have all those custom patterns created. Charge whatever you want and keep it all.

If you only had 100 clients and they only wanted 5 custom patterns each, that's still an opportunity for you to earn another $250K, since 100 clients times 5 positions = 500 patterns, and 500 patterns times $500 = $250,000. Or you could charge them nothing and generate $250K worth of good will, trust, and referrals. It can remain our little secret that we didn't charge you for any of those patterns.

Finally, we can make it possible for you to create and give each of your clients online access to an inventory management system for the employees in each of their companies. It will give them the power to match their people against their custom job patterns and get the information they need to know about what each employee needs, in VERY specific terms. It will help them get employees to perform at higher levels and stay at their company longer. One thing you might not have thought of is this: Because of the time savings it offers alone, an online inventory management system for their talent like this is easily valued at over $2,000 per year.

Let's say you get 100 clients using this system. That's another $200,000 worth of resources we can give to you to share with your clients. This power will help you strengthen your relationships, earn referrals, and deliver value that greatly exceeds what any of your clients pay for your services. Then your clients have no reason to leave.

If you're worried that you or your clients might struggle to learn how to use all this stuff, or that you don't have the time, interest, or staff time available to explain any of this to your clients and prospects, we have you covered there, too.

We have built in step-by-step video training modules that walk clients through everything they need to know in bite-size chunks so nobody gets confused about anything. Sales, service, and training are all done FOR you! We even have a workbook for step-by-step marketing.

It's the exact same training material you and your clients would receive if you paid one of our consultants their daily consulting fees, which start at $5,000 a day plus travel expenses, to go on-site and train an executive team personally. You and your clients get unlimited access to the video training modules for FREE!

Let's face it, some big companies spend more on toilet paper for their facilities each year than it would cost to assess everyone and take inventory of their talent, build custom patterns, and utilize an inventory management system of their talent to make better decisions, faster.

Before sharing any of this with your current or future clients, it is important that you see how many tens of thousands of dollars, hundreds of thousands of dollars, or even millions of dollars your clients can recoup or capture by getting close to, hitting, or even exceeding the reasonable improvement goals they establish when they use the Human Capital Calculator.

Then we want to give you the power to share the tools, training, and technology needed to help your clients reach their goals—and do it in a way that can help you and your firm earn up-front and ongoing residual income too.

As it relates to creating ongoing residual income streams for your business without much, if any, extra effort, we're going to let you in on a little secret. You see, we have skin in the game too, and that's why we need each other.

Why else would we provide all these amazing resources and tools for you to use in your accounting and/or payroll business to help your clients with their existing staff issues without asking you for an arm, a leg, and your firstborn child? Beyond analyzing current employees, when your clients discover the power to find out how an APPLICANT matches (or doesn't match) each seat on their bus BEFORE they hire and invest the time and money TRAINING them, they find that they also have the power to solve ALL KINDS of problems BEFORE THEY EVER OCCUR.

Tony Robbins told a story in his book *Awaken the Giant Within* about a guy who was standing on the shore of a river, when along came a drowning victim screaming for help. The guy dove in, made a daring rescue, and pulled the victim to shore. Of course, he was exhausted, and as soon as he lifted his head, he noticed two more people coming downstream hollering for help. So the guy made two more daring rescues, and as he lay on the beach completely exhausted after rescuing all these people, he noticed four more people coming downstream hollering for help. The moral of the story is this: Had he just taken the time to go upriver and stop the one person throwing all these people in the river in the first place, he would have saved a lot of time and energy by dealing with the single cause of the problem upriver as opposed to the many effects downriver.

That is the beauty of pre-employment assessment. Smart employers know that if they want to reduce turnover, they must hire people who fit the job. They know that if they want to improve engagement, they also need to find ways to reduce conflict and drama. If they want to get more done, they must hire and retain people with a work ethic. If they want to increase sales, they must hire and retain people who can sell. If they want to reduce injuries, they must hire and retain people who don't abuse illegal drugs. If they want to reduce employee theft, they must hire and retain honest people.

When done correctly, employment assessment and pre-employment testing helps solve those problems, upriver, before they occur. When you have the tools, training, and systems to solve those kind of problems for clients, and can offer them a better-than-money-back guarantee that does more than just eliminate their risk, you and your business become a Purple Cow and are NOT like all the other accounting and payroll companies out there.

If you want to remain a brown cow and keep doing what you've always done, we wish you the best but are not really that interested in working with you, and it would probably be a waste of time to engage in a conversation past this.

If this does makes sense to you, we want you to earn your clients' pre-employment testing business in the future, and we are confident you will once you and your clients implement the tools and training we have put into place to make things better within their existing staff. The ongoing residual revenue streams tied to pre-employment assessment are just another reason we think smart accounting and payroll companies will want to add assessments to their offerings.

It's a new and different way for you to help your clients reduce their risk. The margins are higher, and your prospects and customers can't just get these products anywhere. And since we are willing to provide FUTURE pre-employment assessments at wholesale prices to the accounting and payroll companies we choose to form strategic partnerships with, it creates a win-win-win scenario where our firm makes money providing assessments to you at wholesale prices.

Your firm makes money providing assessments to your prospects and clients at retail prices. And your current and future clients capture savings and revenue by dealing with both current challenges and future issues "upriver" that they wouldn't have otherwise.

Since change is a constant when it comes to employment because of growth, retirements, and promotions, putting an employee assessment and pre-employment testing system in place at your client locations is like installing a toll both in their HR office that pays you every time applicants walk through their doors.

And once you see the margins, we're sure you'll agree that the PROFIT is much higher on assessment tools than it is on most, if not all, of your other services—but this isn't an either-or choice. You can offer it all. Think about that. Let it sink in.

Takeaway: What that means to you as a strategic partner is that there will be a continual demand and ANOTHER ongoing stream of passive residual income for you and us. It's a win-win for everyone involved. The cost savings and revenue opportunities you AND your clients capture by working with us that you wouldn't have otherwise make working together a no-brainer. Especially since any investments your clients make in pre-employment assessment services should amount to nothing more than a small fraction of the savings we worked together to help them capture. So we are really just offering you and your clients a better way to do business that pays for itself multiple times over when implemented properly.

If you feel good about what you've read, it sounds like it makes sense, and you'd like to look a little deeper, then we invite you to go to our website (see below) and click on the link where it says "How to Become a Strategic Partner - Click Here" so we can learn a little about you and your firm, too, before we visit.

https://amohumancapital.com/

Chapter 6

The Wrap-Up

I f it makes sense for you to work with us, here is a list and summary of what we can do to help and support you and your business.

For our accounting- and payroll-based strategic partners whom we elect to work with, we will do several things:

- **First**, we will give you the ability to run Human Capital Calculator reports for your clients. Are you worried you won't know what to say or how to present the reports?

  o Don't worry—we have step-by-step guides to walk you through everything you need to say and do to best serve your clients and position yourself as an expert.

  o If you ever did color-by-number pictures when you were a kid, it's kind of like that, but instead of creating a picture, we are creating a sense of urgency that will make your clients want to do more business with you right now without taking up a bunch of your time.

- **Second,** we will give you the ability to use our proprietary online systems to easily help your clients take inventory of the strengths and opportunities for improvement within their existing staff at no charge. You, of course, can use our products and charge as much as you see fit, and keep all associated fees.

- **Third,** you will have the power to help clients identify who is on their bus using the Personality Plus behavioral assessment, and identify what each seat on their bus looks like by creating custom job patterns based on their top performers in each of those positions.

- **Fourth,** you will be granted the power to give clients access to an online inventory management system for their people that can help them improve engagement, performance, and retention of their existing employees AND make better hiring decisions in the future—so they can do it right the first time instead of doing it over. When that happens, you end up with a force field around your client base, and you create up-front and ongoing revenue streams from pre-employment assessment that requires little or no extra effort because the clients and the systems we've built do almost all of the work for you. When you help clients avoid costs and hassles that are exponentially greater than what your professional services cost, it shouldn't be a surprise when they go out of their way to tell others and you get phone calls from prospects you've never met begging you to help their businesses too.

- **Fifth,** you will receive access to "done-for-you" training and marketing resources.

  o Don't have the time or interest in explaining these tools and how to use them to clients? No problem. We have a modular video-based training system that does all that work for you.

  o Don't want to make sales presentations? It's not a problem. It has been our experience that when someone sees the results of their Human Capital Calculator report, they will be begging you for help anyway.

  o For prospects who haven't been exposed to the Human Capital Calculator, we made a video that explains everything for you without referencing our company name or contact information so you can use it as your own on your website, social media, or email marketing. When we say we have done-for-you marketing in place and ready to go, we mean it.

Icing on the cake: As for best practices, if that's not enough, we offer a better-than-money-back guarantee that eliminates the entire financial risk for the end users and our strategic partners who work with them on every project, so there is never anything to have to apologize for or defend. It's a win for your clients. It's a win for you and your firm. It's a win for us. And that's the way it should be.

This isn't something that takes days, weeks, months, or years to pull off. We've already invested the time and spent the money necessary to condense and streamline everything to the essentials.

We feel confident, given all the support mechanisms in place, that we've streamlined things so you can be ready to start helping your clients in a single afternoon. And finally, obviously, it's only fair for all involved that our partners share a significant portion of the ongoing pre-employment assessment revenue while we work behind the scenes to provide support. The good news is that we aren't stingy, and we think you'll find the profit margin on our products to be quite rewarding if we ever get the chance to discuss those numbers.

Imagine what you could do with a BUNCH of new clients! And because our company and platform can support as many new clients as you can add—without you having to add headcount, buy more equipment, or add office space to keep up with your growth—that's just more revenue you can use however you want.

The only thing you'd have to decide then is what to do with the extra revenue. Would you use the extra revenue to hire more people to support the other aspects of your business that are labor-intensive, so you can have more free time or do other things you are passionate about, like spend time with your family or go on vacations? Would you just put it in the bank and take pleasure in watching your account grow? Would you like to make your business more valuable to turn over to your kids someday?

Would you want to be able to command a higher selling price and make your business more attractive to potential buyers? Whatever you decide, it's entirely up to you.

In closing, we need to warn you and make something crystal clear:

This isn't one of those get-rich-quick schemes that promises you fame and fortune for doing nothing. That's not our style, and it's not what we're about.

So here's the scoop. The system we've put together isn't pie-in-the-sky, ivory tower stuff. It's a sensible, prudent, and fundamentally sound strategy supported with step-by-step instruction and all the tools needed to implement it.

In no way are we suggesting or promising that everyone (or anyone) who partners with us is going to make any amount of money. Who knows, you might not even care about making more money because you're making enough already, and you just want to take great care of your clients and solidify—or even expand—your reputation as THE thought leader in your market. And that's OK too. We get it.

That's just our way of saying that we don't have any idea how much you or anyone else who partners with us will make, and that's why we think of it as more of a pilot program. We certainly have goals and believe they can be achieved—otherwise we wouldn't have put all this together.

We are certain little or nothing will change for you, or us, if you become a strategic partner and don't take action and follow the steps and use the tools correctly, but that's pretty much true of anything that's worthwhile.

This isn't like any business-building system for accounting or payroll firms you've ever seen. There's no fluff or filler, just battle-tested strategies, tactics, and tools that have been adapted SPECIFICALLY for your industry.

And it's easy to understand. You can get through it in an afternoon. It's about MORE than just consulting, too. It's easy!

As part of the program, our goals are to collect and analyze feedback from established and growth-oriented accounting and payroll companies looking to add a minimum of $200,000 to $2.5 million a year in extra profit, and we believe it can be done without adding headcount or detracting from your current efforts. If working with us can't result in increasing your PROFITS by $200,000 at a bare minimum for a small firm, and ideally closer to $2.5 million or more per year for a mid-size or larger firm, then we doubt our goals are closely aligned—and that's OK. Even though that means it probably isn't the right time for us to work together, we're glad we were able to share information.

As a bonus, you will have access to our knowledgeable team, who will personally guide you step-by-step through the process. We want every person and company we work with to walk away glad that they know us and feeling like they are better off because they do.

Takeaway: You have nothing to lose and lots to gain. The same goes for your clients. The next step is up to you. Go to our site, click on the link, and answer the questions. We look forward to learning about you and your firm and visiting with you soon. Don't delay. Waiting one day, or one week, might be all the time that is necessary for someone else to slide in and grab the last of the remaining spots in our pilot program. We don't want to be the one who must give you that bad news or put you on a waiting list.

An old mentor of ours once said that indecision is a decision, and the only things that come to those who wait are the leftovers from the people who hustle. He was right.

How does an accounting and payroll firm become a strategic partner and qualify for wholesale pricing, support, and training on the assessment products and services?

Click on the link labeled "How to Become a Strategic Partner" at https://amohumancapital.com/ and answer the questions on the short questionnaire that is presented. We will follow up with you once your information has been reviewed.

Chapter 7

The Workbook

Section 1

How to Grow Your Accounting/Payroll Business

Repeat the steps listed below every month. Engage clients. Build curiosity. Earn more revenue.

Week 1

- Make an announcement—via email, social media, print, dashboards

Week 2

- Post/send out the intro videos listed on the admin links page.

Week 3

- Pick a social media video to send out with a "how we can help" update.

Section 2

Important Administrative Links

In this section you will find video links explaining in detail the BENEFITS for your company, as well as explaining "reverse risk" to your clients. These are easy-to-use "on-demand" tools built in to simplify communication with your team and your clients.

- Use this video link to provide a quick explanation to <u>clients</u>: https://vimeo.com/323866831

- Use this video link to provide more in-depth information to your <u>clients</u>: https://vimeo.com/267714802

- Use this FREE download link to get the PDF of Mason Duchatschek's book *People Matter Most*: https://drive.google.com/file/d/1Z2isJhSjpIKZj h5WwajwO2Is9RWZoEYN/view?usp=sharing

Section 3

Tweets for Twitter / Short Facebook Updates

In this section you will find quick video links offering short, engaging tweets or posts to get the attention of your followers. Using these short posts every 3-4 days will continue to build your online presence and create curiosity.

How can we help you reduce turnover?
https://vimeo.com/331266158

How can we help you reduce workers' comp costs?
https://vimeo.com/331264502

How can we help you reduce employee theft?
https://vimeo.com/331272218

How can we help you increase sales and retain customers? https://vimeo.com/331274423

Want to increase the ROI of your employee engagement efforts? https://vimeo.com/331268682

What are our customers saying?
https://vimeo.com/218837332

Section 4

Letter Content / Website Announcements (Email, Print, Facebook & Blogs)

These are "ready-to-use" marketing messages you can put to use right away. Remember to utilize any and all forms of communication you may have with your clients—dashboards, emails, Facebook direct messages, inserts in mailed invoices, etc. Let people know you are here to be their one-stop shop.

Don't forget to utilize <u>any and all forms of communication!</u>

Announcement #1

<u>Subject:</u>

Announcement: A negotiation on your behalf …

<u>Message:</u>

Great news! We've discovered a new way to help clients that is so valuable it may very well exceed the investment you make in our services each year—many times over.

Contact us today if you or your organization is struggling with any of the following challenges:

1) Increasing sales, productivity, or client retention

2) Reducing employee turnover

3) Minimizing employee conflict and drama

Announcement #2

<u>Subject:</u>

Got sandbaggers?

<u>Message:</u>

I'm not talking about people literally filling sandbags, like if there was a flood or something. I'm talking about employees doing just enough work not to get fired. You know the type.

I'm not saying it's OK, but I understand why this happens, and it could be costing you a FORTUNE. (Hint: It might even be YOUR fault.)

Never fear. We discovered a new way to help clients with this problem.

If this is an issue in your company, reach out to us to find out how to **solve this problem** now and help **prevent it** from happening in the future!

Announcement #3:

<u>Subject:</u>

Customer service training to fix hiring mistakes

<u>Message:</u>

For the sake of discussion, let's say that two new hires go through the exact same customer service training program and learn what to say to difficult customers in different situations.

Unfortunately, HOW they talk to customers can be MORE important than what they say.

Can they take the pressure and work with customers who push their buttons?

What good is customer service training if your reps do what they are supposed to do, but in a way that makes things worse instead of better?

Want to find out which of your employees **have what it takes** BEFORE you put them in positions they aren't cut out for?

If so, reach out to us to find out how to **solve this problems** now and help **prevent it** from happening in the future!

Announcement #4:

Subject:

Fun & Games (until someone gets hurt & YOU have to pay for it)

Message:

What if accidents were as easy to prevent as keeping fire away from gasoline? Well, they are. (Hint: It's not always about safety training.)

Sometimes accident prevention is as simple as making sure good workers don't make bad decisions and show up for work under the influence of drugs or alcohol.

Other times it can be as simple as making sure you put people with calm, organized, and compliant personalities in certain work environments instead of people without these traits.

If you want the power to know how to match people and their personalities with the jobs you have so you can avoid unnecessary injuries, conflicts, and sub-par performance, then I encourage you to **reach out to us** and get access to some new resources we've acquired that can help resolve and prevent these issues.

Announcement #5:

Subject:

How growing people is like planting a garden

Message:

Do you treat your employees like a garden that is your only source of food?

An old-school IBM sales manager named John Hauser once asked same that question. Then he said,

"Growing people is like planting a garden. Start with quality seeds, provide them with nourishment, and give them time to grow."

Think about it. Do you treat the people in your organization like you would a garden that you depended on for your ONLY nourishment and growth?

If not, do you want to know how to do this? Reach out to us to find out how to **solve this problems** now and help **prevent it** from happening in the future!

Section 5

The Assessment Education Series

In this section we have ready-to-use training videos and tools available to ensure that end users are properly trained in implementing and understanding assessments. It is required that the leadership—most typically someone in a human resources role—take the education series and pass a quick test at the end.

P.S. We've included the length of each video so you can plan accordingly!

Introduction (Watch these first.)

Employee Selection Secrets: Strategy and Tactics (11:08)

http://vimeo.com/buildatribe/review/117628859/084d8279dd

Assessment Basics

The Johnston Index Basic Skills Assessment (2:57)

http://vimeo.com/buildatribe/review/117295119/411e9d0fbd

The Insure Survey - The Secrets of Hiring Honest, Reliable Employees With a Work Ethic (8:29)

http://vimeo.com/buildatribe/review/117295117/c13
76af480

The Personality Plus - Training Video #1 (8:36)

http://vimeo.com/buildatribe/review/117295125/1be
212a50a

The Personality Plus - Training Video #2 (8:23)

http://vimeo.com/buildatribe/review/117628858/596
6689eac

Team Master - How to Minimize Conflict, Improve
Performance and Reduce Risk of Lawsuits (8:33)

http://vimeo.com/buildatribe/review/117295139/88b
62cc4eb

Strategy and Tactics

A Way to Introduce the Selection Process to Applicants
and Get Them to Reveal Info They Might Have Tried to
Hide (2:49)

http://vimeo.com/buildatribe/review/117291866/875
f7e589b

The Hiring Funnel - Sample Selection Processes for
Hourly and Salaried Employees (3:56)

http://vimeo.com/buildatribe/review/117376943/12a
9caf9e6

Imprinting - A Secret to Improved New Employee Retention and Performance (5:18)

http://vimeo.com/buildatribe/review/117317494/3b6 364fbb6

Inventory of Talent - How to Manage Your Inventory of Talent (5:29)

http://vimeo.com/buildatribe/review/117291864/6a8 096c25c

Site Functionality / Navigation

Site Tour - Explore the Functionality of Your Scoring Site (11:41)

http://vimeo.com/buildatribe/review/117291865/2e7 3d0caf1

Multi-location Systems - How to Transfer Units and Create Team Master Reports (3:08)

http://vimeo.com/buildatribe/review/117608801/51d 74ffde4

How to Create a Team Master Report (1:54)

http://vimeo.com/buildatribe/review/117317498/5c6 a90be0a

Frequently Asked Questions

Q&A - Frequently Asked Questions (11:47)

http://vimeo.com/buildatribe/review/117317497/eb2c687b49

Section 6

Frequently Asked Questions

1. What do clients get?

They receive:

a. Their own web-based inventory management system for their talent (aka the Hiring Suite)

b. The Personality Plus behavioral assessment for each of their current employees (regularly $60 per employee)

c. Access to Mason Duchatschek's Assessment Education Series, which is a modular online video training system that describes how to maximize the power of the assessments and the inventory management system of talent

d. Creation of custom "success patterns" when significant numbers of top performers are identified by the client and available for any given position

2. What's the "better-than-money-back" guarantee?

Once all employees have been assessed using the Personality Plus, within the next 30 days, if a client doesn't feel their investment was worth exponentially more than they invested, they may receive a 100%

money-back guarantee and they may keep all the assessments of their existing staff, access to training videos, and use of the Hiring Suite online system. The only requirement is that key executives complete the training modules and pass the "certification test" with a score of 80% or better. (It is a 30-question true-or-false test.)

The video at this link explains it in further detail: https://vimeo.com/267714802

3. Are there any additional costs or obligations required of your clients or participants?

No. The focus of this project is entirely on the assessment, development, and management of EXISTING employees in your clients' companies, and the fees for these services have been covered as part of this program.

However, if your clients wish to acquire additional assessments in the future to assess potential job applicants (as part of a pre-employment testing program), then they will have the option to purchase them at that time if they choose. There is NO OBLIGATION TO PURCHASE ASSESSMENTS OF ANY KIND AT ANY TIME.

4. Can your clients have their current employees assessed with the Personality Plus a few at a time or as often as they choose?

No. The assessment of current employees is a one-time offer. As part of this initiative, a client company may receive a Personality Plus assessment (regularly $60 each) for each of the full-time and part-time employees who are on their payroll and have them complete the assessment questionnaire by the assessment scoring date/deadline. The assessment scoring date/deadline is the date the client company specifies as the date by which all current employees must have completed their Personality Plus questionnaire.

5. Can a client request individual assessment results before the results are available for all of the rest of the current employees?

No. When the assessment scoring date/deadline has passed, all current employees who have completed the Personality Plus questionnaire will have their assessments scored together, in one batch.

6. If a few current employees fail to complete their Personality Plus questionnaire before the assessment scoring date, will their results be included in the client company's data at a later date?

No and yes (it depends). Once the assessment scoring date/deadline has passed, every employee who has completed the Personality Plus questionnaire will be scored, and their data will be transferred into the client's inventory management system for their talent (aka the Hiring Suite scoring site). So in this case the answer is no.

However, after the assessment scoring date/deadline has passed, any current employees who failed to complete their questionnaire on time will always have the <u>option</u> of *taking it again at the client's expense.* So in this case the answer is yes, IF the late individuals are willing to retake the questionnaire and the client is willing to pay for each additional assessment.

7. What if a current employee tries to "fake" their results on the Personality Plus or doesn't take it seriously and checks random boxes? Can clients have them take it again, and have the costs covered, too?

This does happen. When it does, it triggers low scores on what is known as the "distortion scale," and this topic is covered in detail in the training videos. If the individual who did this is willing to retake the questionnaire and the client is willing to pay for each additional assessment, then the results can be added to the client's inventory management system for their talent (aka the Hiring Suite scoring site). The costs of having individual employees <u>retake</u> the Personality Plus are NOT covered.

8. Several other assessments are mentioned in the Assessment Education Series, like the Johnston Index (basic skills assessment) and the Insure Survey (measuring integrity, substance abuse, reliability, and work ethic). Are the costs of those assessments included for clients' existing employees too?

Those two assessments are discussed in the Assessment Education Series and are geared toward pre-employment testing purposes. They are also integrated into the Hiring Suite online system. Because each client's initial project is focused on helping them with issues related to current employees, the Johnston Index and Insure Survey are not administered as part of this process.

The Johnston Index and Insure Survey are available to clients who have completed the Assessment Education Series and want to purchase them for pre-employment testing of job applicants in the future.

However, Team Master reports (which are also derived from Personality Plus questionnaire data) ARE available at no additional charge for current employees who completed the Personality Plus questionnaire before the assessment scoring date/deadline.

9. What is the process like?

We take inventory of strengths and weaknesses for each of your client's employees by identifying their suitability to perform different jobs within the company. Inventory is taken by administering a powerful and incredibly thorough behavioral assessment to each employee (the Personality Plus).

We give your clients the option to list key positions in their company and identify the top performers in each of them. For each position where at least 10–15 top performers have been identified, we will compile the statistical data from the top performers that were specified and create a "custom success pattern" to be loaded onto an electronic database/inventory management system of talent (aka the Hiring Suite). For positions where fewer than 10–15 top performers can be designated, an alternative data-gathering method will be used.

This system can then be used to aid in future decisions regarding employee development, management, and promotions, as well as decisions regarding hiring. Think of it as a web-based inventory management system for human resources.

The Assessment Education Series is a web-based video training series provided for all your clients.

10. How does an accounting and/or payroll company become a strategic partner and qualify for wholesale pricing, support, and training on the assessment products and services?

Click on the link labeled "How to Become a Strategic Partner" at https://amohumancapital.com/ and answer the questions on the short questionnaire that is presented. We will follow up with you once your information has been reviewed.

Section 7

<u>Introduction and Presentation Templates</u>

Sample Initial Call Client Template *(if you get their voicemail)*

Hi, Mr. Business Owner, it's Mason over at your CPA firm, and I'm sorry I missed you. Whenever I do work for clients, I make it a point to look for ways to help them recognize every opportunity to save money and spot little problems before they become bigger ones. Anyway … I've been reviewing your books, scrutinizing the numbers, and analyzing the trends, and I've discovered a few things that are causing me concern. I feel the need to schedule a meeting. My number is 314-123-4567.

Sample Initial Call Client Template

Hi, Mr. Business Owner, it's Mason over at your CPA firm. Do you have a minute, or did I catch you at a bad time?

Here's what's going on. Whenever I do work for you, I'm always looking for ways to help you recognize every opportunity to save money and spot little problems before they become bigger ones.

Anyway … I've been reviewing your books, scrutinizing your numbers, and analyzing the Trends, and I've discovered a few things that are causing me concern. We need to meet about it.

How soon could we do that?

Sample Initial Client Meeting Template

Intro:

As I said on the phone, I'm always looking for ways to help you recognize every opportunity to save money and spot little problems before they become bigger ones. Anyway, I've been reviewing your books, scrutinizing your numbers, and analyzing the trends, and I've discovered a few things that are causing me concern.

Just so you know, to stay on top of things, I make a habit of investing blocks of non-billable hours into my client relationships each year, most of the time without them even knowing it. Because I do, my clients typically stay longer and I get referrals without having to ask, so everything works out for everyone in the end.

I realize that when you're the boss, your decisions are only as sound as the facts and timing on which they're based, and no employee wants to bring the boss bad news. When employees have no other choice, they often water it down as a matter of self-preservation.

Here's the thing. The numbers don't lie. The tell a story, and when used the right way, they help you make better decisions faster.

Anyway… here's what I did.

I took your real numbers. I did an analysis of things like employee turnover rates, sales numbers, workers' comp costs, shrinkage/employee theft, salaries, and overtime costs, and put together a report that reveals, as closely as possible, the lost profits and REAL costs to your business—because I used YOUR company's ACTUAL numbers in my calculations. It also showcases potential rewards tied to achievable improvement goals you may want to set in each of these areas.

As a bonus, I've included some research and trends related to your challenges, as well as strategies you might wish to consider employing to fix the issues and capture the opportunities they help you identify.

Let me show you what I found.…

Presenting the report:

There are basically two parts of this report.

Part 1 is the summary page, and it shows you your current costs related to things like employee turnover, employee engagement, workers' compensation, employee theft, and profits tied to sales and customer retention. It also shows your potential savings as well as new revenues that can be captured if you're able to meet whatever reasonable and achievable goals you've set for yourself.

Part 2 breaks down the details of the report, area by area. In some areas, it provides baseline research to benchmark typical costs so you can compare and contrast them with your own.

Best-practice strategies and tactics are also presented so you get access to some new ideas that may enhance or complement your own thoughts about how to achieve the goals you've set.

Let's go area-by-area and see what story the data tells us based on the numbers I entered for your company.

Present area details, one area at a time.

Present the Summary Page.

Offer to help.

<u>Offer to help:</u>

I've got some good news and bad news.

The bad news is right in front of us. There are issues and they are costing you. If someone was embezzling this much money each year, and would continue draining your business until something was done about it, how long would you wait to fix it?

The good news is that our firm has tapped into and partnered with some world-class experts and an incredible set of tools they've developed to address these kind of things.

Have you ever heard of Jim Collins's best-selling book *Good to Great*, where he said the most important thing your business can do is get the wrong people off the bus, get the right people on the bus, and put them in the right seats? The bus Collins was referring to was, of course, your business.

Collins said it is even more important than your businesses strategy, because if you have the right people, and they're in the right seats, they will figure out the right strategy.

Anyway … that book came out in 2001 or 2002 and people are STILL talking about it. I think Collins was right and he made a ton of sense.

Unfortunately, Collins's book didn't tell you HOW to do it, and it didn't mention the TOOLS that were necessary.

Fortunately, the leaders in our firm reached out to a nationwide expert whose expertise picks up where Collins left off, and we developed a relationship with his firm. He's an Amazon.com #1 best-selling author of multiple books, and his ideas have been featured in *Selling Power* magazine, *Entrepreneur* magazine, and

The New York Times. We now have in-house experts who have been certified to use their strategies and tools to better serve our clients.

The best news is that because you're already a client of our firm, and you clearly have some issues that need to be addressed, I feel pretty confident that I can get the other partners of our firm to step up and fund at least a portion of a special project that I believe will absolutely help you with some, if not all, of the issues identified in your report.

Short explanation:

In a nutshell, this project I'm talking about includes access to the tools and training you'd need to make the kind of improvements highlighted in this report.

I will need to share this report and a short application with the powers that be in our organization to see if we can get part of it funded for you. I feel very confident this will happen and a good portion of the costs will be covered—otherwise I would have never brought this up.

I can also get you a link to a video that explains exactly how we could help you overcome these challenges, and that explains things better and faster than I could sitting right in front of you—and because this is so important, I'd hate to leave out anything that might be critical to your understanding or the success of this project.

Longer explanation:

Here's how the project works.

Step 1 is about taking inventory of the people you've got to work with and looking at what you still need in VERY specific terms.

What you'll get is an inventory of the strengths and weaknesses of each of your employees, which identifies their suitability to perform different jobs within your company. This inventory is taken by administering a powerful behavioral assessment to each employee, which normally costs $60 per person. You've got _____ employees, so that's $60 x _____ (# of employees), for a total of $_____, but I'm confident our firm will put some skin in the game and cover half of it if you do. Plus, there's a "better-than-money-back guarantee" that goes along with it, so there's no downside and a huge upside for you and your company.

This behavioral assessment is the tool that tells you if you've got the right people in the right "seats." It also tells you how to turn good employees into great ones by offering SPECIFIC customized guidance on how to surround them with the people, tools, technology, and training they need to perform at a higher level and contribute more to your bottom line.

For any position where you can identify at least 10-15 top performers, you can also use the Statistical data to create a "custom success pattern" for any job you want, so that info can help you in future decisions regarding employee management, development, and promotions, as well as decisions regarding hiring.

Step 2.

You're also going to get a custom-built online website, which is kind of like an inventory management system for your employees. It's the place that stores all of your assessment data. It's also the place where your leadership team gets access to a private step-by-step trainingsystem composed of online videos that show you and your management team exactly how to make better decisions, faster, when it comes to your people.

It's in this training that you're going to learn the secrets of using your new tools and best practices to reduce employee turnover, maximize their engagement, and address the other issues we talked about in your report.

There's only one catch, and it's not really much of a catch because it makes so much sense. It's more like a win-win strategy. This whole project and all the funding is focused on addressing your CURRENT challenges related to CURRENT employees. As you will undoubtedly discover, there are other uses for the assessment tools you will be learning about and using. At some point you're bound to ask yourself, "Could I just use these same assessments on job applicants so I can hire the right people the first time and prevent the kind of issues we're dealing with now from rearing their ugly heads again in the future?"

Of course the answer is yes, and if you want to use those tools in the future, on potential job applicants, so you know what you're getting and don't have to "hire and hope," then you can buy those future assessments on an as-needed basis. There is no obligation, and it's entirely up to you.

First our firm wants to help our existing clients with pressing issues right now, and we're willing invest some of our own resources in clients willing to meet us halfway and follow the system as it is designed.

We want to exceed expectations clients have for our services and earn the kind of loyalty that makes them want to stay clients for a very long time—and also send us referrals without us having to ask.

After the project is completed for current employees, if clients want to invest in our tools so they can use them for pre-employment testing of future job applicants, then that's a new service we are happy to offer. And we are betting that the savings we help clients experience, and the revenues we help them capture that they otherwise wouldn't have, will more than exceed anything they would invest in pre-employment testing services in the future, so the whole idea is to execute a business-improvement strategy that pays for itself in advance.

Sample Application Approach Template (optional)

Like I said earlier, I will need to share your report and a short application. It's online and only has about 10 questions. It should only take 2–3 minutes to fill it out online, and if you go through it with me now, I will go lobby on your behalf to get this project partially funded for your company.

I'm very confident we can get as much as half of the cost of this project funded for the current employees at your company, and secure a "better-than-money-back guarantee" for you as well. I just want to do my part to help you FIRST RECOGNIZE and SECONDLY ADDRESS the issues with your current employees that are right front of us now and need to be addressed right away.

Let's fill this out now....

The Last Resort

If all else fails, or you don't have the time or interest in learning how to use the tools or sending out the "done-for-you" marketing content, there is one last thing you can do to serve the unmet needs of your clients and prospects. Here it is.

Step 1.

Show this video to your clients and prospects. (It has no reference to any other company, phone number, or website, so you can use this promotional video as your own.)

https://vimeo.com/395548051

Step 2.

Ask your prospect/client if there is any step they are willing to risk skipping to save a few bucks.

Step 3.

When they say "no," it means they want help in the areas mentioned, and you can have them contact us and we will take care of them for you.

Thank you and best wishes!

Mason Duchatschek

Jessica Coffey

www.AmoHumanCapital.com